Sports Illustrated KIDS

STARS OF SPORTS

MIKE TROUT

BASEBALL'S MVP

by Matt Chandler

CAPSTONE PRESS
a capstone imprint

Stars of Sports is published by Capstone Press, an imprint of Capstone
1710 Roe Crest Drive, North Mankato, Minnesota 56003
www.capstonepub.com

Copyright © 2021 by Capstone. All rights reserved. No part of this publication may be reproduced in whole or in part, or stored in a retrieval system, or transmitted in any form or by any means, electronic, mechanical, photocopying, recording, or otherwise, without written permission of the publisher.

SPORTS ILLUSTRATED KIDS is a trademark of ABG-SI LLC. Used with permission.

Library of Congress Cataloging-in-Publication Data

Names: Chandler, Matt, author.
Title: Mike Trout : baseball's MVP / by Matt Chandler.
Description: North Mankato, Minnesota : Capstone Press, [2021] | Series: Sports illustrated kids stars of sports | Includes bibliographical references and index. | Audience: Ages 8-11 | Audience: Grades 4-6 |
Summary: "American-League superstar Mike Trout moved through the minors at record speed to become a breakout star his rookie year. From Rookie of the Year to All-Star appearances to record-setting feats and MVP Awards, Trout has earned his place as one of the best centerfielders in baseball history. Is a World Series ring next? Get all the facts on Trout's rise to the top and his future plans in this hard-hitting sports biography."— Provided by publisher.
Identifiers: LCCN 2020037712 (print) | LCCN 2020037713 (ebook) | ISBN 9781496695284 (hardcover) | ISBN 9781977154651 (pdf) | ISBN 9781977156310 (kindle edition)
Subjects: LCSH: Trout, Mike, 1991– —Juvenile literature. | Center fielders (Baseball)—United States—Biography—Juvenile literature. | Baseball players—United States—Biography—Juvenile literature. | Most Valuable Player Award (Baseball)—Juvenile literature.
Classification: LCC GV865.T73 C43 2021 (print) | LCC GV865.T73 (ebook) | DDC 796.357092 [B]—dc23
LC record available at https://lccn.loc.gov/2020037712
LC ebook record available at https://lccn.loc.gov/2020037713

Copyright ABG-SI LLC. Used under license.

Editorial Credits
Editor: Alison Deering; Designer: Heidi Thompson; Media Researcher: Morgan Walters; Production Specialist: Spencer Rosio

All internet sites appearing in back matter were available and accurate when this book was sent to press.

Direct Quotations
Pages 6 and 7, from December 30, 2014, video, "Raising a Young Athlete: Advice from Mr. & Mrs. Trout," https://www.youtube.com
Page 8, from March 27, 2017, *Sports Illustrated* article, "The New Testament: An oral history of Mike Trout's greatest moments to date," https://www.si.com
Page 24, from March 24, 2019, *The Seattle Times* article, "Mike Trout says he's 'an Angel for life' with new contract," https://www.seattletimes.com

Printed and bound in the USA. 3837

TABLE OF CONTENTS

A YOUNG RECORD BREAKER 4

CHAPTER ONE
FUTURE SUPERSTAR 6

CHAPTER TWO
GOING PRO 10

CHAPTER THREE
TEEN TALENT 14

CHAPTER FOUR
AN ANGEL IN THE OUTFIELD 20

CHAPTER FIVE
ANGEL FOR LIFE 24

TIMELINE 29
GLOSSARY 30
READ MORE 31
INTERNET SITES 31
INDEX. 32

Glossary terms are **BOLD** on first use.

A YOUNG RECORD BREAKER

Mike Trout stepped into the batter's box with a chance to make history. It was the bottom of the eighth inning. Trout's team, the Los Angeles Angels, was leading the Seattle Mariners 11–0.

In his first four trips to the plate, Trout hit a single, a double, and a triple. He was a home run away from one of baseball's greatest feats—hitting for the **cycle**.

Mariners relief pitcher Lucas Luetge delivered a breaking ball low. Trout swung for it. He connected with the ball and drove it deep into center field. The ball sailed into the bleachers.

Trout had done it! At 21 years and 287 days old, he set the record as the youngest player to hit for the cycle in American League history.

>>> Trout swings hard during his Major League debut in 2011.

CHAPTER ONE
FUTURE SUPERSTAR

Mike Trout was born in Vineland, New Jersey, on August 7, 1991. His dad, Jeff, was a former professional baseball player in the minor leagues. Trout grew up learning the game from his dad.

Jeff Trout says he and his wife never pushed their son to focus only on baseball. They wanted him to do what made him happy.

"He really enjoyed fishing and hunting at an early age," his dad said. "He played football . . . he played soccer . . . he's played all the sports."

But Trout was a natural at baseball. His dad said he knew there was something different about his son as early as T-ball.

⟨⟨⟨ Trout (center) poses with his family after winning the 85th Major League Baseball (MLB) All-Star Game Most Valuable Player (MVP) Award in 2014.

FACT

As a kid, Trout was banned from playing a baseball-throwing game at the county fair. He won too many prizes.

"He was always a little bit better, a little bit faster than the kids he played with," Jeff Trout said.

HIGH SCHOOL HERO

Trout wasn't an instant star on his high school baseball team. He was nervous the first time he took the field. Trout was only a freshman, and he was joining a **varsity** practice.

His former coach, Roy Hallenbeck, said Trout was making wild throwing errors. "We were going to send him to the freshman group in a day or two if he didn't turn it around," Hallenbeck later said.

Trout worked hard and never gave up. Soon he grew into a superstar on the diamond.

Trout spent his early years as a pitcher and shortstop. He threw a no-hitter in his junior year. In his senior year, he moved to center field. It led to the best season of his life. Trout hit .531 with 18 home runs.

FACT

Trout was so good in high school that he was forced to **switch hit** in order to participate in a home-run derby. Hitting left-handed, he still won the event.

⫷⫷⫷ Trout makes a catch in the outfield during his Major League debut in 2011.

CHAPTER TWO

After his junior year, Trout accepted a baseball **scholarship** to East Carolina University. But thanks to his monster senior season, everything changed.

Trout began to draw large numbers of **scouts** to his games. He was soon seen as a top **draft** pick. In the first round of the 2009 draft, the Los Angeles Angels selected Trout with the 25th pick of the draft.

FACT

A signing bonus is money offered to a new player by a Major League Baseball (MLB) team to get him to join. The highest signing bonus in current MLB history was $8 million, which went to Gerrit Cole in 2011.

>>> Trout (right) poses with Baseball Commissioner Bud Selig after being picked by the Los Angeles Angels in the 2009 MLB draft.

Trout had a decision to make. Should he go to college or straight to the pros? College could give him more time to develop his game. But millions of dollars were waiting for him as a professional baseball player.

In the end, Trout decided to sign with the Angels. His contract paid him a $1.215 million signing bonus. The kid from Vineland had made it. He was a professional baseball player!

MINOR LEAGUE MONSTER

Very few players jump straight from high school to the major leagues. Players usually spend four to six seasons in the minor leagues—or **farm system**—first. Trout was a rare exception. He only played one full season of minor league baseball. He began the 2010 season playing center field for the Rancho Cucamonga Quakes.

Trout quickly moved up the Angels farm system. He jumped two levels in his first minor league season and finished the season playing for the Cedar Rapids Kernels. Combined, the teenager hit .341 with 10 home runs and 58 runs batted in (RBI). Trout also stole an incredible 56 bases.

⟨⟨⟨ Trout attempts to steal a base at Angel Stadium in 2010.

⟨⟨⟨ Trout slides to safety during a Baseball World Cup qualifier game in Puerto Rico in 2010.

Moving on Up

In 2009, the Angels assigned Trout to the Arizona **Rookie** League to begin his professional career. He was only 17 years old. Trout played in just 39 games in Arizona before being promoted to the next level in the minors. He had hit .360 in his first professional experience. In all, he played in only 175 minor league games before making his Major League **debut**.

CHAPTER THREE
TEEN TALENT

Trout got stronger as he began his second year of professional baseball. The Angels promoted him to the AA Arkansas Travelers to start the 2011 season. AA baseball is the second-highest level in minor league baseball. Trout continued to hit for average (.326) and power (11 home runs in 91 games).

Then, in July, Angels center fielder Peter Bourjos was hurt. Trout got the call. He was going to the major leagues!

Trout made his major league debut against the Seattle Mariners on July 8, 2011. More than 40,000 fans packed the stadium. Trout played center field. He made three catches in the game.

Manager Mike Scioscia batted Trout ninth in the order. He wanted to take the pressure off the rookie. But Trout struggled. He went hitless in three at bats.

⋘ Trout (right) takes the field in his Major League debut against the Seattle Mariners.

ROCKY ROAD

Trout's time in the majors was short lived. After hitting just .163 in 12 starts, he was sent back to AA Arkansas.

Trout worked hard in the minors. He wanted to get back to the majors and prove himself.

On August 19, 2011, he did just that. The Angels brought Trout back to California. The rookie hit a home run in his first night back.

⟨⟨⟨ Trout (left) is congratulated by a teammate during a game in Arlington, Texas, in 2011.

⋘ Trout sits in the dugout during a 2011 game against the St. Louis Cardinals.

Trout remained with the Angels for the rest of the season. But in 40 games, he only hit .220. He stole just four bases.

Despite his struggles at the plate, Trout showed flashes of the power, speed, and defense fans expected. Many believed 2012 would be his breakout year.

ROOKIE OF THE YEAR

Trout was expected to make the Angels **roster** in 2012. But after arriving at spring training, he got the flu. The rookie spent much of spring training sick. He lost 23 pounds. The virus cost him his spot on opening day.

⟨⟨⟨ Trout bats against the Texas Rangers during a 2012 game.

Instead, Trout began the season at AAA Salt Lake, one step down from the majors. But he continued to improve. In his first 20 games, Trout hit .403.

Then, less than a month into the season, the Angels called. This time, Trout was great from the start. He hit for power. He stole bases. He dazzled fans with his catches in center field.

Trout dives to catch a fly ball at Angel Stadium.

Trout finished 2012 with a .326 average. He led the American League with 49 stolen bases. Trout crushed 30 home runs and scored 129 times. He was named the American League Rookie of the Year.

FACT

Trout received $20,000 for winning the Players Choice Rookie of the Year Award. He donated the money to his high school baseball team to improve their field.

CHAPTER FOUR
AN ANGEL IN THE OUTFIELD

For the first time in his young career, Trout didn't have to worry about making it to the majors. He arrived at spring training in 2013 as the reigning Rookie of the Year. He was the Angels' starting center fielder.

Trout was ready for a strong season. He hit .323 that year. He finished with 27 home runs and 97 RBI. He led the American League in walks in 2013 with 110.

⋘ Trout scores against the Detroit Tigers in 2013.

Thanks to his ability to get on base, Trout also led the league in runs scored. It was a trend that continued. He led the American League in runs scored for three years in a row.

FACT

Trout grew up idolizing New York Yankees player Derek Jeter. When the Angels played the New York Yankees, Trout asked Jeter for his autograph in the middle of the game!

Trout's skills paid off. In 2014, he earned a contract extension from the Angels. It was for six years and $144.5 million.

⟪⟪⟪ Trout signs autographs for fans before a spring training game.

That same year, Trout reached a career high with 36 home runs. He led the American League with 111 RBI. Combined with his defensive skills, it was enough to win Trout his first American League Most Valuable Player (MVP) Award.

MOST VALUABLE PLAYER

Trout continued to set records in 2015. On April 17, 2015, he faced off against Houston Astros pitcher Roberto Hernandez.

With the game tied 1–1, Trout hit a fastball into the seats for a two-run home run. With the home run, Trout became the youngest player in history to hit 100 home runs and steal 100 bases.

The next year was yet another strong one for Trout. In 2016, he collected his second MVP Award. For the past five years, he had either won or come in second in the MVP voting.

Trout is considered by many experts to be the greatest five-tool player in baseball. He was a rare player who hit for power and average while having speed, strong fielding skills, and a great arm.

⟨⟨⟨ Trout poses during a spring training photo shoot.

⟨⟨⟨ Trout watches from the dugout during a game against the Houston Astros.

MVP, MVP!

The Most Valuable Player Award is one of the biggest individual awards a baseball player can win. Only 31 players in the history of the game have won the award more than once. Trout collected three American League MVP Awards before turning 29.

CHAPTER FIVE
ANGEL FOR LIFE

Trout was having another strong spring training in 2019. In 17 games, the Angels slugger crushed three home runs and drove in 13 RBI. But his biggest win came in his new contract with the Angels.

Angels owner Arte Moreno had called Trout "everything you want as a leader and a player in your organization." He signed Trout to one of the largest contracts in North American sports history—12 years and a record $426.5 million.

Trout immediately began to earn his contract. That year was one of his biggest seasons. He hit a career-high 45 home runs and drove in 104 runs. His season was so strong that Trout earned his third MVP Award. That was despite missing 28 games during the season.

Trout's contract also says he can't be traded to another team. He will be nearly 40 years old when it expires. That means he will likely play his entire career with the Angels.

◁◁◁ Trout won his third MVP Award in 2019.

HEADED TO THE HALL?

Trout has accomplished so much on the baseball diamond. He has made the All-Star team every year of his big-league career. He is an MVP candidate year after year and has won the award three times.

⋘ Trout (right) poses with Los Angeles Angels team owner Arte Moreno and his wife, Carole.

⋘ Trout shakes hands with Angels owner Arte Moreno while receiving his 2016 MVP Award.

But there is one drawback. So far, Trout has been unable to lead the Angels to a World Series title. In Trout's first eight years, the Angels have only made the playoffs once. They were swept in the 2014 American League Division Series. Trout went 1–12 in the series, hitting just .083.

Trout is undoubtedly a superstar. If he stays healthy, he will be a lock for the Baseball Hall of Fame when he retires. But superstars are expected to carry their team to the playoffs. If Trout can't find a way to help the Angels win one, his **legacy** may suffer.

WHAT'S NEXT?

Willie Mays, Joe DiMaggio, Ken Griffey Jr., and Mickey Mantle are some of the greatest baseball players to have played center field. Will Mike Trout have a place on that list when his career ends? His statistics say he will.

If he stays healthy, Trout will have nearly 3,000 hits. He will have hit more than 600 home runs. And his defensive gems will continue to pile up. Right now, Mike Trout is the best active center fielder in the game. Only time will tell if he becomes the greatest of all time.

⟪ Trout stands at the plate during a game against the Boston Red Sox.

TIMELINE

1991 — Mike Trout is born on August 7, in Vineland, New Jersey.

2008 — Trout throws a no-hitter pitching for his high school team.

2009 — Trout graduates from Millville Senior High School in New Jersey.

2009 — The Los Angeles Angels draft Trout with the 25th pick of the MLB draft.

2011 — Trout makes his Major League debut on July 8.

2011 — Trout hits his first Major League home run on July 24 on the road against Orioles reliever Mark Worrell.

2012 — Trout becomes the first player in history to hit 30 home runs, steal 45 bases, and score 125 runs in a season. He wins the Rookie of the Year Award.

2013 — Trout hits for the cycle against the Seattle Mariners on May 21. His 111 RBI lead the American League for the season.

2014 — Trout wins his first American League MVP Award.

2016 — Trout wins his second American League MVP Award.

2019 — Trout picks up his third MVP award and signs the richest contract in the history of Major League Baseball. The new deal is for 12 years and $426.5 million.

GLOSSARY

CYCLE (SAHY-kuhl)—hitting a single, double, triple, and home run in the same game

DEBUT (DAY-byoo)—a player's first game

DRAFT (DRAFT)—the process of choosing a person to join a sports organization or team

FARM SYSTEM (FAHRM SIS-tuhm)—the minor league teams that develop players to play in the major leagues; each minor league team is connected to a major league team

LEGACY (LEG-uh-see)—qualities and actions that one is remembered for; something that is passed on to future generations

ROOKIE (RUK-ee)—a first-year player

ROSTER (ROSS-tur)—a list of players on a team

SCHOLARSHIP (SKOL-ur-ship)—a grant or prize that pays for a student to go to college or to follow a course of study

SCOUT (SKOWT)—someone who looks for players who might be able to be professionals

SWITCH HIT (SWICH HIT)—to bat right-handed against a left-handed pitcher and left-handed against a right-handed pitcher in baseball

VARSITY (VAHR-si-tee)—the main team that represents a school or club in contests

READ MORE

Burrell, Dean. *Baseball Biographies for Kids: The Greatest Players From the 1960s to Today*. Emeryville, CA: Rockridge Press, 2020.

Chandler, Matt. *Baseball's Greatest Walk-Offs and Other Crunch-Time Heroics*. Mankato, Minn: Capstone Press, 2020.

Rajczak, Michael. *The Greatest Baseball Players of All Time*. New York: Gareth Stevens Publishing, 2020.

INTERNET SITES

Los Angeles Angels Official Site
mlb.com/angels

Mike Trout on Major League Baseball Site
mlb.com/player/mike-trout-545361

Mike Trout's Career Statistics
baseball-reference.com/players/t/troutmi01.shtml

INDEX

AA baseball, 14, 16
AAA baseball, 19
All-Star team, 26
American League, 4, 19, 20–21, 23, 27
Arizona Rookie League, 13
Arkansas Travelers, 14, 16

Baseball Hall of Fame, 27
Bourjos, Peter, 14

Cedar Rapids Kernels, 12
Cole, Gerrit, 10

DiMaggio, Joe, 28

East Carolina University, 10

farm system, 12
five-tool players, 22

Griffey, Jr., Ken, 28

Hallenbeck, Roy, 8
Hernandez, Roberto, 22
Houston Astros, 22

Jeter, Derek, 21

Los Angeles Angels, 4, 10–11, 12, 13, 14, 16–17, 18–19, 20–21, 24–25, 27
Luetge, Lucas, 4

Major League Baseball, 10, 12–13, 14, 16, 19, 20
    draft, 10–11

Mantle, Mickey, 28
Mays, Willie, 28
minor league baseball, 6, 12–13, 14, 16
Moreno, Arte, 24
Most Valuable Player Award, 21, 22, 23, 24, 26

New York Yankees, 21

playoffs, 27

Rancho Cucamonga Quakes, 12
Rookie of the Year, 19, 20

Scioscia, Mike, 14
Seattle Mariners, 4, 14
spring training, 18, 20, 24

Trout, Mike
    contracts, 11, 21, 24–25
    early life, 6–7
    family, 6–7
    high school career, 8, 10
    Major League debut, 14
    records, 4, 22, 24
    signing bonus, 10–11
    stats, 8, 12, 13, 14, 16–17, 19, 20–21, 24, 27, 28

Vineland, New Jersey, 6, 11

World Series, 27